What Did We Do?
Before
Streaming Music

by Samantha S. Bell

FOCUS
READERS®

BEACON

www.focusreaders.com

Focus Readers is distributed by North Star Editions:
sales@northstareditions.com | 888-417-0195

Produced for Focus Readers by Red Line Editorial.

Photographs ©: Everett Collection/Shutterstock Images, cover (left), 1 (left); Rawpixel.com/ Shutterstock Images, cover (right), 1 (right), 26; KSC/NASA, 4; Sigitas Kondratas/Shutterstock Images, 6, 29; Vadim Orlov/Shutterstock Images, 8; Everett Historical/Shutterstock Images, 11; Natalia61/ Shutterstock Images, 13; chonticha stocker/Shutterstock Images, 14; richardjohnson/Shutterstock Images, 16–17; Nataliia Chubakova/Shutterstock Images, 18; Early Spring/Shutterstock Images, 21; C3620 Siegle Jochen/Deutsch Presse Agentur/Newscom, 22; David MG/Shutterstock Images, 24

Library of Congress Cataloging-in-Publication Data
Names: Bell, Samantha, author.
Title: Before streaming music / by Samantha S. Bell.
Description: Lake Elmo, MN : Focus Readers, 2020. | Series: What did we do?
   | Includes index. | Audience: Grades 4-6
Identifiers: LCCN 2019035441 (print) | LCCN 2019035442 (ebook) | ISBN
   9781644930458 (hardcover) | ISBN 9781644931240 (paperback) | ISBN
   9781644932827 (ebook pdf) | ISBN 9781644932032 (hosted ebook)
Subjects: LCSH: Phonograph--History--Juvenile literature. |
   Sound--Recording and reproducing--History--Juvenile literature.
Classification: LCC ML1055 .B42 2020 (print) | LCC ML1055 (ebook) | DDC
   621.389/33--dc23
LC record available at https://lccn.loc.gov/2019035441
LC ebook record available at https://lccn.loc.gov/2019035442

Printed in the United States of America
Mankato, MN
012020

About the Author

Samantha S. Bell is a children's writer and illustrator. She has written more than 100 nonfiction books for children. She streams music on her phone, but she still has some CDs and cassette tapes.

Table of Contents

Chapter 1

Moon Tunes

In July 1969, a spacecraft blasted off into the sky. Three astronauts rode inside. They were traveling to the moon. Reaching the moon took three days. Along the way, the astronauts listened to music.

 The Apollo 11 spacecraft lifts off from its launch pad in Florida.

 Most cassette tapes can hold between 60 and 90 minutes of music.

They played **cassette tapes**. Each astronaut had a tape of his favorite songs. Some songs were about the moon.

People still listen to music when they go on trips. But most people no longer use cassette tapes. Instead, millions of people stream music. All they need is a device that can access the internet. Then they can play thousands of songs right from a phone or tablet.

Fun Fact

Other astronauts have played cassette tapes on missions, too. They floated around in the spacecraft and danced to the music.

Chapter 2

Music Anytime

People began recording music in the late 1800s. At first, they used phonographs. A needle pressed into wax **cylinders** to record or play sounds. By the early 1900s, people had begun using records.

 Records made it easy for people to listen to their favorite music.

These flat discs had grooves on both sides. Early records held one song on each side.

Before streaming music, radio was the main source for finding new songs. In the 1930s, many radio stations began to focus on one kind of music. Some played classical

Fun Fact

Early records held three minutes of music per side. Many pop songs are still approximately three minutes long.

 Early radios often had fancy wooden casings.

music. Others played jazz or folk songs. People listened to stations that played their favorite **genres**.

They bought records of songs they liked. That way, they could listen to the songs over and over.

In the 1940s, companies began making records that could hold more songs. The LP record is one example. Each side of this record holds approximately 25 minutes of music. That means one record can hold a whole **album**.

By the 1950s, many people had TVs in their homes. Famous musicians began performing on TV.

RECORD PLAYER

The record spins.

The tonearm moves to place the stylus over the record.

The stylus is the needle that touches the record's grooves.

These shows gave people another way to hear music. In fact, some people still listen to music this way.

In the 1960s, cassette tapes became available. Their magnetic tape wound around two small reels.

 After listening to one side of a cassette tape, users flip it around to play the other side.

Music played as the tape went from one reel to another. To start or stop it, people pressed buttons on a cassette player. They could also fast forward or rewind. But they had to guess where each song started.

Tapes held more songs than records. Plus, people could record music from one tape to another. They could also record music from the radio. People often put many songs they liked onto one tape. It was called a mixtape. Friends often shared mixtapes with one another.

Fun Fact

A record has two sides, A and B. Songs on the B side are often less famous. Bonus songs are still called "B sides."

Jukeboxes

In the mid-1900s, many stores and restaurants had jukeboxes. These large machines played music. Customers could choose songs they liked. In the 1950s, each song cost 10 cents to play.

Each jukebox had a list of songs it could play. People put a coin into the machine. Then they picked a song from the list. Motors and **gears** moved the correct record into place. Then the record started to spin.

Many jukeboxes had clear glass in the front. People could watch the record as it played. After the song ended, the machine put it back.

On many jukeboxes, colored lights flash as music plays.

Chapter 3

Music Anywhere

By the early 1970s, many cars had cassette players. People could play tapes while driving. Boom boxes were also popular. People carried these large tape players around. They often played music outdoors.

 Many people brought tape players with them on walks or runs.

However, some people wanted more control over what music they listened to. So, in 1979, Sony introduced the Walkman. This small tape player came with headphones. Its size made it easy to carry. And headphones meant only one person heard the music.

Other inventions also helped people find and store music. In the 1980s, people began using compact discs, or CDs. Like records, CDs are flat and round. But CD

 The shiny side of a CD reflects lasers to play music.

players use **lasers** to read and record music. CDs soon began to replace cassette tapes. Compared to tapes, CDs have better sound. They don't wear out as quickly. And people can easily skip to the songs they want to hear.

 In 2005, Apple released a small MP3 player called the iPod Nano.

In the late 1990s, people began buying MP3 players. These devices store music as **digital** files. People can **download** the songs they want.

They don't need **physical** copies. And they can buy specific songs rather than a whole album.

In 2001, Apple began making MP3 players called iPods. These devices became very popular. Each iPod could hold many songs. People could bring their music with them wherever they went.

Fun Fact

Along with music, iPods can hold photos and videos. Users can also play games.

Chapter 4

Music Today

By the mid-2000s, some people had begun streaming music. They no longer had to download music. Instead, they could use streaming services. These programs send **data** right to a person's device.

 Spotify is a streaming service that allows users to play music on their phones or computers.

 Today, people have many ways to play and share music with friends.

Then the device can play any songs the user wants.

Some streaming services cost money. Others let people listen for free. Like many radio stations, free services often have ads. But people can still choose from thousands of songs. They can try new bands or genres.

Streaming makes finding new music easier than ever. Some services even predict songs users might like. Users can also share songs or playlists with friends.

Fun Fact

By the late 2010s, people in the United States spent more than 30 hours a week listening to music.

Before Streaming Music

Write your answers on a separate piece of paper.

1. Write a sentence describing one way people listened to music before streaming services became common.

2. Do you prefer owning music or streaming music? Why?

3. What method of recording music was invented first?
   - **A.** records
   - **B.** cassette tapes
   - **C.** CDs

4. How did people find a certain song on a cassette tape?
   - **A.** They had to start and stop the tape to find the song.
   - **B.** They pressed a button to skip to the song.
   - **C.** Marks on the tape showed where each song began.

5. What does **focus** mean in this book?

In the 1930s, many radio stations began to focus on one kind of music. Some played classical music.

    A. give more time to one thing
    B. do many different actions at once
    C. shine a light in a dark space

6. What does **predict** mean in this book?

Streaming makes finding new music easier than ever. Some services even predict songs users might like.

    A. change
    B. ignore
    C. guess

Answer key on page 32.

Glossary

album
A group of songs a musician releases and sells as a set.

cassette tapes
Small cases holding magnetic tape that can be used to record or play sounds.

cylinders
Objects that are shaped like tubes.

data
Information represented by numbers, especially for computers.

digital
Having to do with information used on a computer.

download
To send data from one computer system to another.

gears
Wheels with teeth that perform a specific function in a machine.

genres
Types or categories of something.

lasers
Devices that produce a very intense, narrow beam of light.

physical
Related to things that can be touched or held.

To Learn More

BOOKS

Burgan, Michael. *Spotify, Pandora, and Streaming Music.* Broomall, PA: Mason Crest, 2018.

Colby, Jennifer. *Phonograph to Streaming Music.* Ann Arbor, MI: Cherry Lake Publishing, 2019.

Jackson, Tom. *Music Technology.* Tucson, AZ: Brown Bear Books, 2015.

NOTE TO EDUCATORS

Visit **www.focusreaders.com** to find lesson plans, activities, links, and other resources related to this title.

Index

C
cassette player, 14, 19–20
cassette tapes, 6–7, 13–15, 19, 21
CDs, 20–21

D
data, 25
downloading, 22, 25

I
iPods, 23

J
jukeboxes, 16

M
mixtapes, 15
MP3 players, 22–23

P
phone, 7
phonographs, 9
playlists, 27

R
radio, 10–11, 15, 26
records, 9–10, 12–13, 15, 16, 20

S
streaming services, 25–27

T
tablet, 7
TV, 12

Answer Key: 1. Answers will vary; **2.** Answers will vary; **3.** A; **4.** A; **5.** A; **6.** C